The Dynamite Book of Ghosts and Haunted Houses

by **Margaret Ronan**

Illustrations by Arthur Thompson

A Dynamite Book from Scholastic Paperbacks

The Book You Are Holding Is 100% Dynamite!

Yes, Dynamite Books come to you from the same scintillating scribblers and peerless pen-and-inkers who bring you Dynamite Magazine every month: Jane Stine, Series Editor; Greg Wozney Design, Art Direction; Sharon Graham and Judy Gorman, Production Editors; Susan Hood, Assistant Editor; and the whole Hot Stuff gang!

ISBN: 0-590-30622-7

12 11 10 9 8 7 6 5 4 3 2 1   5   0 1 2 3 4 5/8

Printed in the U.S.A.

Table of Contents

Housewarming

When Mabel Wells moved to Cleveland, she picked the house on Decauter Street because it was small and fairly new. Mabel's husband had died the year before, and now there was only herself and her 15-year-old daughter, Kathy. The house had only five rooms, but Mabel felt that was enough.

It turned out to be more than enough.

Once she had moved in, Mabel found that someone had done some do-it-yourself fixing up. The walls of Kathy's room had been covered with imitation wood paneling. It had been stapled in place, and some of it was beginning to pull loose.

"As soon as I can afford it, I'll have that ugly stuff pulled down," Mabel promised. "Then we'll put up some nice wallpaper."

"Good," said Kathy. "It gives me the creeps."

Since they had no friends in Cleveland, Mabel and Kathy never thought of having a house-warming. They got one, anyway. It started in the middle of the night on November 6th.

Mabel was awakened by her daughter's voice. Kathy was standing by the bed, trembling.

"Get up, Mama. I think the closet in my room is on fire."

Mabel stumbled out of bed and went across the hall to Kathy's room. She couldn't smell smoke, but she could see a red glow shining under the closet door. But when she yanked the door open, the closet was dark. There was no sign of a fire.

Two nights later, Kathy woke her again. This time the girl was calling from her room.

"Mama! The walls are hot!"

Mabel ran to Kathy's door. She started to turn the knob, then yanked her hand back with a cry. The knob was too hot to touch!

She wrapped a bathtowel around her hand and managed to turn the knob. Kathy was cowering in the middle of the room. Very carefully, Mabel reached out to touch the nearest wall. It was scorching.

When the fire department came, they found no fire. They had to agree that the walls and door of Kathy's room were scorching — too hot to put a bare hand on. But the rest of the house was perfectly normal.

The next day, electricians came to check the wiring of the Wells' house. Perhaps there was an electrical fire smoldering behind the walls. There wasn't. Everything was fine. Kathy's room stayed hot for two more days. Then it cooled back down to normal.

But some other things weren't so normal. Four days later, Mabel decided to do the family washing. She was halfway through the job when the skies outside clouded up. Mabel hurried, figuring she might be able to get the wash out on the lines and dry before it rained.

With Kathy's help, she hung out the wash in record time. But an hour later, it began to drizzle. Mabel dashed out to take down the wet clothes before they got wetter.

It wasn't as much of a task as it might have been. On the two lines where Kathy's clothes had hung, there was now nothing dangling from the clothespins but charred scraps! Somehow, those wet clothes had managed to burn up.

Puzzled, Mabel gathered up what was left of the wash and took it indoors. Since it was still wet, she would have to hang it on the lines in the basement. But she finished the last line just in time to see the clothes on the first line begin to smolder. A minute later, several of the garments there burst into flames.

Trying not to scream, Mabel threw buckets of water over the burning clothes. Then she took down the remaining wash and piled it in the tub. With shaking hands, she filled the tub with water. Would all that water keep the clothes from catching fire? She wasn't sure.

At dinner, she told Kathy what had happened to the wash.

"There's no reason for it," she kept saying.

Kathy frowned. "Maybe there is. What do we know about this house, anyway? I'll bet you didn't know that there's a hollow space in back of the closet wall in my room."

"How do you know it's hollow?"

"By the way it sounds when you knock on the wall. Do you think it's a secret passage or something?"

Mabel shook her head. "Houses this small don't have secret passages. There's probably a space there because the room has been repaneled."

But why had it been repaneled? she began to wonder. She asked the agent who had rented the house to her. After some hesitation, he replied, "Well, the truth is that there was a fire in that room several years ago. Funny thing — that room was gutted, but the rest of house was all right. Why do you ask?"

"We've been having some problems with the room," was all Mabel would tell him. She had already decided to pull down the paneling at the back of the closet. It didn't make sense, but she felt she had to know what lay behind it.

The next day she and Kathy armed themselves with heavy gloves and work tools. The job was easier than they expected. The back panel of the closet was flimsy, and they had it down in no time.

The wall behind was badly scorched.

"That must have been some fire!" Kathy exclaimed. "I wonder if anyone was hurt."

Suddenly Mabel felt a rising panic. It was a feeling that she had never experienced before. It seemed to her that if she didn't get out of that closet, she would die!

"What's the matter?" Kathy asked, staring at her. "You're white as a sheet!"

"I have to get out! Let me out!" Mabel heard herself screaming. She dropped the tools and ran out of the room. Kathy ran after her.

"What happened?" she asked her mother.

"I don't know," Mabel gasped. "I was never so afraid in my life. But I'm sure something terrible happened in that room, and I mean to find out what it was. Otherwise, we won't ever have any peace in this house."

She went back to the renting agent. "I want to know more about that fire you told me about," she said.

At first he didn't want to talk about it. "It happened a long time ago. What has it got to do with the present?"

Mabel was firm. "I think it has a lot to do with whether or not we go on living in that house."

Finally the agent gave in. "It was a bad fire, but the fire department got it under control fast and kept it from spreading to the rest of the house. What I didn't want to tell you was that a child died in it — a boy of six. He had been locked in the closet as a punishment, and the flames kept anyone from getting to him."

"Thank you for telling me," said Mabel. "When I came here, I was so upset that I planned to cancel my lease. But now that I understand what happened, I think it's important for me to go on living there."

"I don't understand," said the agent.

"It's all right," Mabel answered. "My job now is to make that poor child understand."

She went back home and told Kathy what she had learned. "I think I know what to do," she said. "You change rooms with me. Then we'll take the door off that closet. Maybe then that poor little ghost will know it has a way out."

Although Kathy didn't like the idea of her mother sleeping in the bedroom, Mabel insisted. She was no longer afraid. And if taking the closet door off didn't work, she wanted to be there where the boy had died.

"Maybe I can talk to him and tell him everything is all right now," she said. "At least I can try."

Did her plan work? It must have. Mabel still lives in the little house, and sleeps in the small bedroom. And there hasn't been a fire there since the washing burned up on the clothesline.

———————————

The House
That Was
Never Finished

Sarah Parlee had never been to a fortune-teller, but her friends all spoke highly of this one.

"You're going to be married soon, Sarah," Francine Perkins had told her. "Aren't you the least bit curious about your future?"

That was why Sarah was standing outside the little house in New Haven on a spring morning in 1862. The house was shabby, and so was the old woman who invited her to come in. But it was Sarah — well-dressed and well-bred — who was nervous when they sat down with the glowing crystal ball between them.

What the old woman had to tell her didn't make her less uneasy.

"The man you marry has a heavy burden," said the fortune-teller. "He will pass it to you. The souls of those his family has wronged cry out for revenge."

"It's all nonsense," Sarah told herself as she hurried away from the shabby house. "No one can see into the future. Besides, what has William's family ever done to anyone? They're very nice people."

If Sarah had thought a little more deeply about her fiance's family, she might not have been so sure. William Wirt Winchester, the man she would marry in a few weeks, was the son of the inventor of the famous Winchester repeater rifle.

In 1862, the War Between the States was still raging. Bullets fired from Winchester rifles had killed both Union and Confederate soldiers. In the West, the Winchester rifle was regarded highly. It could slaughter buffalo and Indians with equal ease.

But Sarah didn't think of this. And she soon forgot the fortune-teller's warning. No one was going to scare her out of marrying William. And no one did. The wedding took place as planned.

Four years later, a baby girl was born to Sarah and William. But a week later, the infant died. It took Sarah a long time to get over the shock.

She was just beginning to feel well and strong again when her husband became ill with tuberculosis. On March 7, 1881, he died. He left Sarah 20 million dollars. She was rich, but she was terribly alone. Life seemed to close in around her, walling her up in a prison of grief.

For months she would see no one, and she went nowhere. Finally, a group of her friends took action. They brushed past her servants and demanded to see Sarah.

"If you go on this way, you'll become ill," they told her. "Go to another place and start a new life. Leave New Haven, where you've known so much unhappiness."

"My place is here, where my husband and daughter are buried," she replied sadly.

"If you stay, you'll soon join them, Sarah. William wouldn't want you to spend the rest of your life mourning him."

Sarah burst into tears. "If only I knew what he would want me to do!" she sobbed.

One of the women spoke up timidly. "I know you don't like fortune-tellers," she said, "but there's a man in Boston they say can talk to the spirit world. His name is Adam Coons and he is said to be quite amazing. Why don't you go to see him. Perhaps he can help you."

Sarah took her friend's advice and went to Boston. With a heart full of misgivings, she made an appointment with Adam Coons. She did not tell him her name or anything about herself. Yet Coons described William's appearance perfectly.

"Your husband is in this room," Coons told Sarah. "I see him standing beside you. He wants me to tell you that he loves you and is always near you."

Then Coons' voice grew harsh. "But he sends you this warning. You will be forever haunted by the ghosts of those killed by Winchester rifles. You must sell all your property and leave New Haven. Then you must search for another house where you can make amends."

"But how will I know which house?" Sarah faltered.

"You will know it when you see it. Buy it at once. Then make sure there is room enough in it for all those wronged spirits. As long as you build for the spirits, you will live."

Sarah seemed convinced that this strange message had really come from her husband. She did just what she had been told to do. She sold her property in New Haven, packed up, and began to wander across the United States — looking for the right house. In San Jose, in the Santa Clara Valley of California, she found it.

It was a 17-room house standing on 130 acres of land. The house was still being built for a Dr. Caldwell. But with her millions, Sarah was able to offer him a price he couldn't refuse. She bought the house and set about the task that she believed would free her from the Winchester curse.

"Build and build," Coons had told her. Sarah hired workmen and carpenters. She had them add 10 more rooms, then 26. Rooms were built around rooms. Some rooms had no windows.

One of these windowless rooms was located on the second floor of the house. It was a small, secret chamber, known as the Blue Room. No one but Sarah was allowed to enter it. But she went there every night. Then she would put on a special long robe and sit down to wait for the spirits to visit her. To call the spirits, she had a bell tower built.

The bell rang each night at midnight, then again at 1:00 and 2:00 A.M. Sarah hired two men whose only job was to ring the bell by pulling a rope which ran to their quarters in the basement.

While Sarah tried to make peace with the spirits of those killed by Winchester rifles, sales of those same rifles kept on bringing her over a thousand dollars a day. She spent it on the house. For 36 years, 22 carpenters hammered away — day in, day out. The house grew to 160 rooms. It was seven stories high. Eighteen servants kept the place spotless. And 12 gardeners turned the surrounding acres into a park, hidden from outsiders by hedges so high that only the towers of the house showed over them.

As the house grew bigger, it also grew weirder. Some doors opened on blank walls. One stairway was built inside a closet — and went nowhere. Often windows were built on walls between rooms. It was not unusual to open a closet door — and find just a wall behind it. Or to start up a staircase that stopped at the ceiling.

Sarah's house had 47 fireplaces. But the

number that really seems to have fascinated her was 13. The windows had 13 panes. The walls had 13 panels. There were 13 cupolas on the greenhouse, and 13 palm trees along the driveway. Only one staircase had more than 13 steps. It had 42, but each step was only two inches high.

Did Sarah order her house built this way because she was crazy? Or did she hope to make it so confusing that those vengeful spirits wouldn't be able to find their way around in it?

Although Sarah slept in a different bedroom every night, her favorite room was called the Daisy Room because of the flower patterns in its stained-glass windows. But when the great San Francisco earthquake struck on April 18, 1906, the Daisy Room almost did Sarah in. The quake made the top three floors of the house collapse, and the ceiling of the room fell in — trapping Sarah. When her servants finally dug her out, she swore never to enter the Daisy Room again. She had it boarded up.

For Sarah, the earthquake proved to be a blessing in disguise. It gave her an excuse to keep on building. More rooms were added, more chimneys sprouted up. Alone in the Blue Room at night, Sarah drew plans of the work she wanted done the following day. She believed the directions for these plans came from the spirits.

The builders must have wondered about those plans. But Sarah paid such high wages that nobody questioned her orders — even when it meant building chimneys that weren't even connected to fireplaces, and skylights in the middle of floors.

"As long as you build, you will live," Sarah had been told by Adam Coons. But all the carpenters she hired couldn't keep death away forever. On September 4, 1922, Sarah Winchester died in her sleep. She was 83.

Margaret Merrium, Sarah's niece, inherited the mystery house. For many years she kept it as Sarah had, then sold it to a company that has opened it to visitors as a "Mystery House." Today the Winchester Mystery House is a California Historical Landmark. Visitors who go over the house will find they have traveled a mile and a half — without going outside.

After Sarah's death, the Daisy Room was opened again. It is said to be haunted. Some visitors have reported feeling a "block" of cold air there, the size of a human being. And on one occasion, the room was felt to shake violently — just as it did the night the ceiling fell, trapping Sarah under the beams.

The Cellar Door

In the foothills of West Virginia there is a house that was once haunted by the ghost of a skunk.

You might expect a skunk's ghost to announce its presence with an unpleasant smell. But that's not the way it happened in this house.

The house was built by a retired storekeeper named Elbert Mercer. Elbert's father had recently died, leaving his son five acres of rocky hillside. In Elbert's opinion, his small yellow frame house brightened up the landscape.

On a November day in 1936, Elbert moved in with his sister, Doris. She was a widow and had volunteered to keep house for her brother.

On her first Monday in the house, Doris went down into the basement to do the week's washing. She had no washing machine, so she set to work to scrub everything on a board in the big stone tub beneath the cellar window.

She was halfway through the chore when something moving outside the cellar window caught her attention. The sun was coming directly through the window, so at first she couldn't see clearly. She got the impression of a small shadowy bulk. Then, like a photograph developing, the shadow seemed to form itself into the shape of a skunk.

Doris squinted at it for a moment. Then her wet hands flew up to her mouth in dismay. The animal was having convulsions. She could hear it bumping against the glass as it thrashed and twitched.

Quickly, Doris ran upstairs. Her brother was sitting at the kitchen table, reading a newspaper.

"Elbert, hurry!" Doris gasped. "There's a skunk right by the cellar window. It looks as if it's in terrible pain."

The two ran around to the back of the house. "There!" said Doris, pointing to the small writhing shape by the window. But then she stopped in astonishment. The shape of the skunk was becoming blurred. It seemed to shrink down into a dark blot, then disappear.

"What in the world . . ." Elbert began. But Doris had already swung around and was pointing at the entrance to the cellar steps. It was covered by a slanting wooden door.

"Did you see that?" she said. "It ran under the door."

"The skunk?" Elbert asked in bewilderment.

"No, the white thing," Doris replied.

Elbert stared at her. "I think you must have a touch of sun. I'm not sure what I saw under the window, but nothing could get under that door. I fitted it myself. You couldn't even slide a piece of paper under it! You'd have to open it first, and you can see that I put a good strong bolt on it."

"But I saw it," Doris insisted. "It was like . . . like part of an apron . . ."

Elbert tried hard to make his voice calm and soothing. "Now, now. We've both been working pretty hard on the house. We're just getting spooked because we're tired. Come on inside. I'll fix us both some lunch and we'll feel better."

After lunch, Doris was willing to admit that she must have been "seeing things." She even felt able to go downstairs and finish the washing.

Once down there, she checked the cellar door from the inside. Elbert was right. It fit so tightly that not even a piece of paper could have been shoved under it.

But the memory of what she had seen wouldn't go away. She dreamed about it night after night. Strangely enough, the dreams didn't frighten her. Not even the one she had that caused her to sleepwalk.

In the dream, she was again washing in front of the cellar window. She looked up and saw the contorted body of the skunk. Then it pressed against the window, and she saw that its small face was human — the wrinkled, frightened face of an old man.

At that moment she heard a voice behind her. "It will soon be over," it said. Doris turned and saw a woman standing on the cellar steps. She wore a long dark dress with a white apron tied over it. In one hand she held a glass of liquid.

Doris awoke with a shudder. She was standing in the cellar. Moonlight streamed through the window, but she was alone.

As she worked around the house, she thought about what had happened. She became certain that the skunk, the white thing, and the dream were all part of a puzzle. She was also sure that if she could find out what it meant, it would never bother her again.

"I feel that I've been looking at bits of a picture," she told her brother. "If I can fit them together, I'll see the whole picture. I'm sure it has something to do with this house."

Elbert shook his head. "You always had too much imagination. How could your spooks have anything to do with this house. It's brand-new. Ghosts hang around old places — if there are ghosts, which I don't for a minute believe."

"But you saw the skunk disappear," Doris told him.

"I don't know what I saw. Some optical illusion, probably. If I were you, I'd put the whole thing out of my mind."

"I can't. Maybe the answer is something about the land the house is on. When did Pa buy it? Who did he buy it from?"

Elbert sighed. "He bought it in 1895. Picked it up cheap. Nobody had paid taxes on it for years. There was nothing on it but some kind of tumbledown shack. Nobody had lived in it for ages, but there was a story going around that it had been some kind of an inn once."

"How could I find out about the inn?"

"You might try Alice Bryan at the Charleston library. Local history is a hobby of hers. If anybody knows about the inn, she does."

The next day Alice drove to Charleston and went to the library. She wondered if Alice Bryan would think she was crazy when she heard about the "spooks." Well, it didn't matter if everyone thought she was out of her mind. She soon would be, unless she solved the mystery.

Miss Bryan listened without a flicker of expression to Doris's story. Then she said, "What is it you want to know? I'm not sure I believe in ghosts."

"I never used to," said Doris. "But it wasn't like seeing ghosts. It was more like getting a message — or pieces of a message. I just feel the answer has something to do with an old inn that used to be on our land."

Miss Bryan stared at her. Then she opened a large drawer and took out a map of the county. "Show me exactly where you and your brother live," she told Doris. When Doris pointed out the spot, she nodded. "I had a hunch that was it. What you call an inn was really two adjoining log houses. They had a connecting passage between them. The passage ran underground, but steps led up from it into each house."

Miss Bryan went to a shelf and took down an old book. She looked in the index and then turned to a page. "Here is an old drawing of the houses. They were owned by a man named Elfron Bethune. He and his wife lived in one and lodged overnight travelers in the other."

"What happened to the Bethunes?" asked Doris.

"I'm surprised that you've lived around here all these years and never heard about it. It was quite a scandal in its day. It seems some travelers never got out of the place. Mrs. Bethune poisoned them, and then Mr. Bethune robbed and buried them. Then she finally poisoned old Elfron. She told all about the other murders at her trial."

Doris felt her heart beginning to pound with excitement. "The pieces all fit together! The white thing I saw was Mrs. Bethune's apron — she wore it in my dream! Before she killed her husband, she tried the poison out on a skunk."

Miss Bryant smiled. "Well, I suppose it's possible that you have gotten some kind of message from the past. Have I made you feel any better?"

"Yes," said Doris. "Now I know what to do."

But she had to wait several weeks for the chance to do it. She thought each Monday might be the day, when she went into the basement to wash. But time went on, and nothing out of the way happened.

Then one afternoon she was raking leaves at the back of the house. A sudden scuffling noise made her look toward the cellar window. The leaves that had drifted under the window were scattering about.

She put down the rake and walked slowly over. She knew what she would see. The skunk was there, rolling around in pain. Then the animal's image began to blur, and Doris looked quickly at the cellar door. She knew now what the flash of white was that seemed to snake under the door.

It was the edge of Mrs. Bethune's apron string.

"It's all over, Mrs. Bethune!" Doris called out loudly. "It was over a long time ago. You paid for what you did. You don't live here anymore. You don't live anywhere."

When Doris tells people about this experience, she always ends her story the same way. "She must have heard me, because nothing strange ever happened in the house again. Do you think that she didn't know she was dead? Do you think she had to relive the moment she decided to kill her husband over and over — as a punishment?"

What do you think?

The Girl Who Was "Witched" Away

On a bitter night in the early 1800s, a man flung open his bedroom window and leaned out. The howling wind drove snow into his face, but he didn't seem to notice.

"Lottie!" he called. "Lottie, is that you?"

The wind was the only answer, but he didn't close the window. There! He saw it again — a flash of red among the snowdrifts. Lottie had worn a red cape the night she vanished. Without putting on a coat, he ran downstairs and out into the storm.

Five feet from the open door, he stopped. The snow before him was marked by a girl's footprints. But the footprints were red, as if they had been painted in blood.

"Lottie!" the man called in despair. He knew no one would answer. Whatever had made those footprints was no longer alive on earth.

The man was Elihu ap Enken, owner of the Wild Goose Tavern in New London, Connecticut. Twenty years before, Elihu had left the Yale farm at Litchfield where he had worked since childhood. In his pocket was every penny of the wages he had earned. He was only 18 then.

In those days, Elihu had only one wish. He wanted to own a tavern on the seacoast. But he knew he needed more of two things — experience and money. He got them both by taking jobs at every inn he came to. No job was too hard or too menial for Elihu. He cleaned, cooked, and served. He worked as a carpenter and blacksmith's helper. He fetched and carried for travelers and stabled their horses.

Five years went by before Elihu could buy his own place. He called it the Wild Goose.

Running a tavern suited Elihu. He liked meeting and talking to all kinds of people. The travelers who came and went brought him news of far-off places. Sometimes they also brought an air of mystery into the Wild Goose. For example, there was the veiled woman who came one night carrying a baby girl in her arms.

The woman rented a room and took the baby upstairs. But in the early morning, she crept out and rode away on a horse that had been tied to a tree at the edge of the woods. She left the baby behind. She also left a note:

"Dear Elihu,

"You did not recognize me. I am Emma Yale. You did not know it when you were a boy at our farm, but we are cousins. Now in my wretched state I leave my daughter in your care. Be kind to her and provide for her. I am going to England."

Elihu did as Emma asked. He adopted the baby, called her Lottie, and raised her as his own. He could not have loved her more if she had been his own.

Lottie turned out to have a heart as kind as Elihu's. As a child, she "adopted" every stray cat and dog. As a teenager, she kept the poor and sick in the neighborhood supplied with food and medicine. It was a common sight to see her, wrapped in a red cloak, carrying baskets of provisions around the neighborhood.

One morning when Lottie was hurrying along the edge of the woods, a bony hand came out between the tree trunks and seized her arm. Lottie found herself swung around to face an old woman. The woman's clothes hung in rags about her, and her stringy hair half covered her face. When she smiled, Lottie saw her broken, blackened teeth.

"What have you got in the basket, my pretty?" asked the hag, still clutching the girl by the arm.

"Food. Some liniment for Granny Soames' bad leg. Some salve for the Goodwin boy's sores," Lottie replied calmly.

The hag grinned. "Nothing for Old Dreary?"

Lottie pulled her arm free and opened the basket. "Take what you need," she said.

Old Dreary peered in the basket, then shook her head. "None of this. It's rum I need! You bring me some from the Wild Goose. I live in the old house near the turnpike. I'll wait there for you. Don't keep me waiting long."

When Lottie got back to the inn, she told Elihu what had happened.

"There'll be no rum for that old devil!" he said. "And you must promise not to go near her house. It's nothing but a ruin. Should have been pulled down long ago."

Lottie was only too glad to promise to stay away from the old woman. Something about Old Dreary frightened her. But two days later, the hag turned up at the back door of the Wild Goose. She jumped at Lottie when the girl came out to get water from the well.

"You shouldn't have made me wait," she hissed. "I want rum. Get it for me now, or I'll make you sorry."

Lottie screamed and Elihu suddenly appeared in the doorway. He shoved Old Dreary away from the girl.

"Take your hands off my daughter!" he shouted. "Never come near her or this house again, or it will be you who's sorry."

Old Dreary backed away. She stretched out her long claw-like fingers at Elihu. "Enjoy today, innkeeper," she jeered. "You won't have many happy days left!" She hobbled away into the woods. Long after she was out of sight, they could hear the echoes of her cackling laugh.

"Maybe you shouldn't have spoken to her that way," said Lottie. "Some people do say that she's a witch."

Elihu put his arm around her shoulders. "Non-sense. There's no such thing as witches. She's just a crazy old woman. To give her rum would only make her worse."

A few days later, Lottie was invited to a party at the Danby house. It was only a short walk for the girl, and Elihu gave his permission. Because the evening was cold and windy, she put her red cloak over her new dress before setting out.

She never returned to the Wild Goose. Nor did she show up at the Danby house. Somewhere on that short dark walk, Lottie vanished into thin air.

Frantic, Elihu organized a search party. They scoured the woods and the countryside. They checked each farm and house for miles around. There was no trace of Lottie.

The first place to be searched, of course, was the tumbledown house of Old Dreary. The drunken old woman was taken off to the jail for questioning. But after a few days they let her go.

"It wasn't me who witched her away," Old Dreary mumbled over and over.

Months later strange whispers reached Elihu. People were saying that Lottie had been seen in the woods, hurrying along in her red cape. But when anyone tried to get near her, she vanished.

Could Lottie still be alive? Elihu almost dared to hope so. Perhaps she had lost her memory. He took two stable boys and searched the woods himself. They found nothing.

Then on that winter night, a kitchen maid came running to Elihu.

"I saw Miss Lottie outside!" she said

breathlessly. "She was running about in the snow!"

And that was why Elihu opened his window to call Lottie's name. That was why he ran out in the snow, just in time to glimpse a flash of red that might have been a girl's cloak. He would have followed the red-rimmed footprints, but the driving snow covered them up.

Two days later, hunters took shelter from a storm in a brush-filled cave near Saybrook. To keep warm, they began to gather the brush to make a fire. Under it lay what was left of Lottie, wrapped in the shreds of a red cloak. She had been dead for months.

To this day, no one knows how she got there — or why she disappeared between the Wild Goose and the Danby house. Both her arms were broken, but there was no clue as to how she died.

Some people say that Lottie is still trying to get home. They claim that on snowy nights she comes back to the spot where the Wild Goose once stood. Then red footprints appear in the snow, leading into darkness.

———————————

The
Haunted Church

In upstate New York, not far from Kingston, a "For Sale" sign hangs outside an empty church. The price is low, but nobody seems willing to buy it. The building has been for sale for a long time. Perhaps that's because people say it is haunted. They claim that at dusk, a white face with eyes like prune pits can sometimes be seen behind the broken windows.

The problems began in the 1950s. Up until then, the church had been a busy, bustling place. On Sundays people came to worship. On weekdays, the minister let local groups use the big basement room for meetings and gatherings.

Mrs. Amelia Garson was den mother for the Cub Scouts in 1952. She was in the church basement about five o'clock on a Wednesday afternoon. The troop had come and gone, and she stayed behind to clean up.

Dusk was falling when she finished. She was putting on her coat when she heard footsteps on the floor above. Thinking that Mr. Cardle, the minister, had come back, she hurried upstairs.

The church was empty. But a moment later she heard the sound of footsteps rushing back and forth.

"They came from behind the pulpit," she remembers. "I thought maybe one of the boys had gotten back in and was playing there. So I marched right up the aisle to put a stop to that!"

Near the pulpit, Mrs. Garson stopped and let out a shriek. A figure dressed in black suddenly leapt out at her. It moved so fast that she couldn't be sure whether it was a woman or a man in a long black coat. But she never forgot its chalk-white face and sunken, black eyes. Or the long, bone-thin arms reaching out at her.

She was too scared to move. "But just as it got near enough to touch me, it vanished! One minute it was there — the next it wasn't."

When Mrs. Garson got home, she was so shaken that her husband wanted to call the police.

"The police can't help," she insisted. "What I saw was a ghost. Call the minister and tell him to come over."

When Mr. Cardle arrived, she told him what had happened. He shook his head. "There are no such things as ghosts," he said. "And even if there were, what would a ghost be doing in church? Some trick of the light made you think you saw someone. After all, it was getting dark and there were lots of shadows."

"What I saw was no shadow," said Mrs. Garson stubbornly. "And I heard it running, too."

A few weeks later, another member of the congregation also got a scare. Lee Groves, the church organist, came in on Saturday afternoon to practice. His playing was interrupted by the sound of laughter.

Groves swung around on the bench and peered down the aisle. It seemed to him that someone dressed in black was sitting at the back of the church.

"Can I help you?" he called out.

The figure didn't answer, but began to laugh again. Mr. Groves thought that perhaps the intruder was drunk.

"If you don't feel well," he shouted, "please leave." Then he began to play again.

The laughter got louder. Groves looked around and saw that the figure seemed to double up on the seat. It was rocking back and forth, overcome by giggles.

Groves became angry. He got up and walked down the aisle.

"This is a house of worship," he said. "If you can't behave properly, please leave."

As he said this, the figure seemed to gather itself together. Then it appeared to expand and

surge toward him. Its strange white face was only inches from his. He could see glistening tear stains on its cheeks. Then it was gone.

But Groves was sure of one thing. "It was the face of an old woman. And she was in terrible distress!"

The following Sunday turned out to be the last time there would ever be a crowd in the little church. As Mr. Cardle began the service, a sudden commotion broke out in the gallery that ran across the back of the room. Everyone present heard the sounds of running footsteps and crazy laughter.

The congregation turned around to see who was making so much noise. What they saw turned their curious expressions into expressions of horror!

The black-clad figure came floating out of the gallery. As it moved up the aisle, it seemed to be at least two feet off the floor. Its arms were thrust out before it, its hands turned palms-upward. A strange, hissing whisper came from it.

"Don't turn me out," it seemed to be saying. "Don't send me away."

By now many people were screaming. One man, braver than the rest, made a grab for the floating figure. His hand passed right through it.

Again the penetrating whisper came. "If I must go, all must go." And a moment later, the ghost was gone.

On the Sundays after that, fewer and fewer people came to services. Those who did come paid little attention to the service. They seemed uneasy and nervous, as if waiting for something to happen. Finally, the minister called a meeting in the auditorium of the local high school.

"As you all know," he told the crowd, "our congregation has been disrupted by some unexplained happenings in our church. In the hope of putting your minds at rest, I have been doing some investigating. I've checked old records and read old newspaper accounts. Here is what I have found out.

"As most of you know, our church was built 30 years ago on the foundation of another church which burned down. It seems that one of the parishioners of the old church was a woman named Kate Brade. She was a deeply religious person, and did many good works in the community.

"Then a sad thing happened. Kate's mind became unbalanced. Her personality changed. When she came to church, it was to disturb the worshippers by laughing or running up and down the aisles.

"People felt sorry for the old woman. They remembered what a good person she had been. For these reasons, they tried to put up with her for a long time. But finally her presence was too disturbing. A vote was taken, and Kate was asked to leave the church forever. She did — but not as people expected. She got into the bell tower one night and hanged herself.

"It may be that the figure we have seen is the unhappy spirit of Kate Brade. Whatever it is, we should all pray that it finds rest."

The congregation regrouped. For months they came to services and prayed as Mr. Cardle had asked. But they were often interrupted by the bell in the church tower. It would begin to ring wildly. But when Mr. Cardle went to investigate, no one was ever there.

Nothing Mr. Cardle could do seemed to help. He gave up, and services were moved to another building. The haunted church was put up for sale.

When I last passed that way, it was still there, forlorn and empty. Or was it empty? I didn't stop to find out.

Julie
and
<u>Walking Otto</u>

Julie Burnett was 10 when she came to live with her Aunt Elsie in New Orleans. It was a bad time for Julie. Her parents had been killed in an automobile accident. Neighbors had come to the Burnett house, packed everything up, and put Julie on the train with a note pinned to her coat so that her aunt could pick her out when she got off at the railroad station.

The sight of Aunt Elsie's house on Garondelet Street did nothing to raise Julie's spirits. It was small and dark. Julie's room was a gloomy place on the second floor.

"I remember thinking that I would never be happy there, never make friends," she recalls. "I was wrong."

But at first it seemed that she was right. The house stood at the end of the street. All the other buildings were stores or warehouses. There were no neighbors with children. The summer stretched ahead, hot and lonely.

Because the house was stuffy, Julie spent a lot of time sitting on the front steps. That was how she first saw Walking Otto.

She heard him before she saw him. She didn't hear footsteps, but the sound of heavy sticks thumping along the sidewalk. Then the old man came into view. He moved stiffly but quickly. When he saw Julie, he swept off his hat and bowed to her.

"Good morning, young lady. My name is Walking Otto. You wouldn't think it to look at me, but I'm 80 years old and I've got two wooden legs. Every day I walk 10 miles. Why don't you join me? You could use the exercise."

His face, smiling at her, was as brown and wrinkled as a walnut. Julie couldn't help smiling back.

"I'll have to ask my aunt," she said.

To her surprise, Aunt Elsie said yes. "Old Otto? Yes, he's harmless. He lives in the shack near the marsh. People say he used to have money, but he's poor as a church mouse now."

After that their walks became everyday events. Julie would listen for the sound of Otto tapping along the sidewalk. Then she would hurry downstairs to meet him at the gate. Thanks to Otto, she began to learn about New Orleans.

"There are more ghosts in this town than any-where else in the U.S.," the old man told her. "Lots of bad things happened here in the old days. There were slaves then, and some of those poor souls were owned by terrible people. They say there are empty houses where you can hear chains rattling and people screaming all night long. But those people have been dead a long time."

There was a pattern to Otto's walks. On Mondays and Fridays, he and Julie went to the wharf and fished for crayfish. Twice a month they walked to the post office, where Otto would be handed a thick envelope with German stamps on it.

"What do you suppose is in the envelope?" she asked her aunt. "Old Otto never says."

"I can't imagine," said Aunt Elsie. "Talk is that Otto came from Germany when he was a young man. Maybe he has relatives there. Maybe they send him money. But if they do, he doesn't seem to spend it. Maybe he buries it under his shack."

"Is it true you have money buried under your shack?" Julie asked Otto the next time she saw him.

He laughed. "So you've heard that rumor," he said. "No, young lady, there is no money there. But there will always be fools in this town who believe such stories, more's the pity."

One afternoon when Julie came back from her walk, Aunt Elsie had visitors. One was a thin, middle-aged woman with bright blonde hair.

The other was a thick-set young man with a sullen face.

"Julie, this is Mrs. Knacken and her son, Peter," Aunt Elsie said. "They want to ask you some questions."

Mrs. Knacken smiled at Julie with thin lips. "We understand you are a friend of old Otto's, Julie. Well, we are his friends, too, although he won't admit it. In fact, we are his cousins."

Julie found this hard to believe. There was something about these two that made her uneasy. But she nodded, and Mrs. Knacken went on:

"Now, Julie, I think you can help us help poor Otto. He won't see us, so you give him this message. There is no reason for him to live in that awful shack. We want you to tell him he is welcome to come and live with us."

For the first time, Peter Knacken spoke up. "The old fool could be living in a fine house, and us with him. He's got plenty of money."

"No, he hasn't!" Julie burst out. "He's poor."

Mrs. Knacken smiled. "No, dear, our cousin Otto is a miser, I'm afraid. Every month he gets a letter from a bank in Germany. He owns property in Europe. There is no reason for him to live like a pauper — except that he's crazy. But I won't have him sent to an institution. I'll take care of him."

Aunt Elsie interrupted. "I'm afraid Julie knows nothing about all this. She'll pass on your invitation to Otto the next time she sees him. But I'm afraid that's all I can permit her to do."

The next day Julie told Walking Otto about Mrs. Knacken and Peter. He snorted and said scornfully, "Those two vultures! I'm ashamed to be related to them. And I'm even more ashamed that they bothered you and your aunt."

"They seem to think you have lots of money," Julie said timidly.

Otto laughed. "What do I need money for? I don't pay rent. I grow my food, or catch it off the wharf. Come along, we'll take a walk to one of my favorite places. I don't take everyone there — only very special young ladies."

The "special" place turned out to be an old graveyard. Many of the stones were sunk flat in the earth. Beside one grave there was a large, round flat stone.

"Sit down on that, Julie," Otto told her. "I hauled that here myself. It took me quite a time to do it, but it's my own special, front-row seat. Don't you forget where it is, now. It's a very important stone."

"Aren't you scared to come here?" Julie asked.

"You mean because it's a graveyard? No, the dead can't hurt you. It's some of the living you have to watch out for, Julie. This is a good place to come to sit and think. I give you my permission to come here and sit on my stone whenever you want to be alone."

It was the last walk they ever took together. Old

Otto didn't turn up the next morning. Two days later, his body was found in a pond near his shack. He had been stabbed and then drowned.

Peter Knacken took some workmen to the shack and had it torn down. Then he ordered the men to dig up the property. Julie watched from her bedroom window. Just as Old Otto had said, there was no money there. She began to cry. Money didn't count. What counted was the fact that she would never see Otto again.

Then the rumors started. People said Otto's ghost had been seen walking around what was left of his little garden. They said he kept his hands pressed over his chest, where he had been stabbed.

One rumor was that Otto was looking for his buried money. Maybe he would point it out. At night people began to come down Julie's street, on their way to try to catch sight of the ghost — and maybe the treasure. Peter Knacken was always in this crowd.

After a while the ghost-hunters got tired and gave up. Walking Otto disappointed them by never showing up, and besides, the weather had turned cold and rainy.

One night Julie awoke to the sound of heavy rain pounding on the rooftop. She was half-asleep, and a strange thought came into her head.

"Poor Otto. He's out there all alone in the cold. He doesn't even have a shack to shelter him anymore."

She got up and took the blanket off her bed. Then she went out in the rain to find Otto.

But when she got to the place where the shack had stood, there was nothing to see but the dark and the rain.

"Otto," she called, "I've brought you a blanket."

A glow appeared in front of her. It seemed to move up from the ground and form itself into a wavering shape. It grew more solid, and she could see that it was Otto. His body wavered on the wooden legs. His hands were pressed against his chest, but he smiled at Julie.

"Put the blanket around yourself," he said. "I don't feel the cold. Let's go for a walk."

Neighbors found Julie the next morning, curled up on the round flat stone in the old cemetery. When they brought her home, her aunt burst into tears.

"We've been looking for you all night!" she cried. "Whatever made you go out in that rain? You've probably caught your death of cold."

"No, no, I'm all right," Julie said earnestly. "I went for a walk with Otto. He told me Peter killed him, and to go tell the police all about it."

Her aunt stared at her. "You must have a fever. You're delirious."

"I'm not, Aunt Elsie. We have to tell the police. He stabbed Otto with a knife with a big nick in the blade. The knife is in a drawer in his room at his house. Otto told me where to find it."

Somewhat dazed, Aunt Elsie went with Julie to the police station. The officer on duty found Julie's story as hard to believe as her aunt had. But when they searched the Knacken house, the knife was there — just where Julie said it would be. Peter was there, too. He broke down and admitted he had murdered Otto.

"I only wanted the money," he kept saying. "It was mine by rights. But the old fool wouldn't tell me where it was."

The day after Peter was arrested, Julie went back to the cemetery. She sat down on the round stone.

"I did what you told me to, Otto," she whispered.

She was never sure whether she really heard the whisper, or only imagined it. It said: "Push back the stone. Dig under it."

Wondering, she looked around. There was no one nearby. She got up and tugged at the stone. Finally she managed to push and shove it to one side. Then she began to scoop away the damp earth that had been under it.

Her fingers were bleeding when they touched the little waterproof pouch with the drawstring top.

Inside there were 50 one-hundred-dollar gold pieces, and a square of tree bark. On the bark, Otto had painted these words:

"For Julie, in memory of those walks. From her friend, Walking Otto."

———————

The Cottage on Clarkson Street

No place ever looked less haunted than the cottage on Clarkson Street in Denver, Colorado, but the people who lived there had a strange story to tell!

Fred and Ella Thompson were newlyweds when they moved into the cottage in 1934. In 1940, they moved out. The cottage was for rent. People moved in, but no one stayed.

When Helen and Jay Pittman saw the cottage, they thought they had found the bargain of the year. But they couldn't understand why the rent was so low.

"The rental agent was only asking $40 a month for a five-room house in good shape," Helen says. "But we didn't quibble or ask questions. We should have."

After the Pittmans moved in, they didn't even have time to meet their neighbors. They painted and plastered the rooms. They put up curtains and put down carpets. They cut the grass, and planted flowers.

As the rooms grew more cheerful, the house seemed to come back to life. "All but the basement," Helen remembers. "It was such a glum place. We whitewashed it and put in some extra lighting fixtures. Jay set up a Ping Pong table down there. But it was never cheerful. The corners always seemed full of shadows. It made me nervous."

Helen tried to stay out of the basement as much as possible. But one afternoon she let Jay talk her into a game of Ping Pong.

"It will be fun," he said.

At first it was. Then suddenly the game was interrupted. A bright-red rubber ball smashed into the center of the table.

Helen and Jay stared at it. Where had it come from? The basement windows were open, but they had screens in them. The door at the top of the stairs was closed.

"It must belong to some kid," Jay said. He reached out to pick it up. The ball rolled away and dropped off the table. Then it rolled into the shadows in a corner.

"Somehow, neither of us wanted to go and hunt for it," Helen says.

The Pittmans tried to go back to their game. But they had to give up. They couldn't help glancing at the corner where the ball had disappeared.

Two afternoons later, Helen was washing dishes in the kitchen. "I had the radio on, but I began to hear another noise," she recalls. "It was a steady thud, thud, thud, and it came from the basement. It sounded exactly as if someone were bouncing a ball.

"The basement stairs led down out of the kitchen. I suddenly felt afraid. I ran over and bolted the basement door shut. The thudding stopped. Then it started in again. Only this time, whatever it was was bouncing from step to step on the basement stairs!"

Jay made a search of the basement. This time he took a flashlight and shone it in each corner. There was no ball.

Helen began to wonder if she had imagined the whole thing. But she didn't wonder long. The next night, the Pittmans were having supper in the kitchen. They both heard it: thud . . . thud . . . thud . . .

"Somebody's down there!" Jay said. "I'll bet it's some neighborhood kid. I'm going to put a stop to it."

He got up and started for the basement door. Helen screamed. Something was bouncing up the basement steps. Then it hit the other side of the door with great force.

"It took us two days to pack up and move out," Helen says. "In all that time, the sounds of a ball being thrown against that door never stopped. But neither of us went near the door. We were too afraid."

When the moving van had driven away, they took the keys back to the rental agent.

"I hoped you two would stay. But nobody stays," he said.

"Why? What do you know about that house?" asked Jay.

The agent looked uncomfortable. "I suppose you are leaving because of the red ball. Some tenants complained that they couldn't get any sleep because they could hear it bouncing all night. One man said every time he went in the basement it bounced out and hit him. Did the neighbors tell you about the Thompson boy?"

Jay and Helen shook their heads.

"No?" asked the agent. "Well, the Thompsons were the first tenants. Tommy, their little boy, used the basement as a playroom. He used to stand at the top of the stairs and bounce his ball all the way down. . . . That's how the accident must have happened."

"The accident?" Helen whispered.

"Yes, the poor child fell — all the way to the bottom of the steps. Broke his neck."

No one rented the cottage on Clarkson Street after the Pittmans left. Three years later, the land it stood on was sold. Workmen came with bulldozers to tear the cottage down. Sometimes their work was interrupted. From out of nowhere, a red rubber ball would bounce into their midst. They could never find out who threw it. Strangely enough, they could never lay hands on the ball, either. It just seemed to disappear into thin air. At least that's the way the story goes.

The Shaking House

For 20 years, Molly Lawson worked as a housekeeper for old Jason Muldoon. She cooked and cleaned and nursed him when he had a stroke. She hoped that when he died, he would leave her the Muldoon house.

It was an old house in the Montana uplands. Muldoon built it when he first came West in the late 1800s. He was engaged to a rancher's daughter then, and he hoped they would marry and have a big family. But the engagement was broken, and Muldoon ended up with a big empty house. The only woman who ever lived there was Molly.

Jason Muldoon died in 1949. He didn't leave a will. But he did have next of kin, his nephew, Hartley.

When Hartley heard of his uncle's death, he left Philadelphia, where he worked in a law firm, and came out to Montana. Molly was still living in the house. Hartley got the idea that she thought the house should be hers. He told her to get out.

"I'll admit I think I earned the right to this house," Molly said, "but you're the next of kin. All I ask is that you let me stay on and keep house for you. You see, this place is the only home I've ever had."

But Hartley didn't agree. "You've got 12 hours to pack and move out," he told her. "I don't need a housekeeper, and if I did, it wouldn't be you."

"You're making a mistake," said Molly. "No one but me will ever rest easy in this house."

When the 12 hours were up, Hartley came back to the house. He brought along the town marshal, in case Molly gave him any trouble. But Molly was all packed and waiting in the hall. She had her coat and hat on.

The marshal knew Molly and liked her. "It wouldn't hurt if she stayed on a few days and helped you get sorted out, would it?" he asked Hartley.

"I think she should leave," said Hartley. "I want the place to myself."

"I'm going," said Molly, "but I'll tell you one thing — you won't ever have this house to yourself."

"Are you threatening me?" Hartley sneered.

"That will be enough, folks," said the marshal.

"Okay, Molly, I'll drive you to Butte, if you want."

"You can drive me down to Kirby. I'll pick up the two A.M. train there when it stops for water," Molly replied.

"But you don't want to wait six hours in the cold. . ." the marshal began. But Molly just picked up her suitcase and marched out to his car. They drove off, and Hartley slammed and locked the door.

Maybe it was the strangeness of being in a new place. Maybe he was just overtired. But Hartley didn't sleep well that night. All over the house floors creaked as if they were being walked on. About two in the morning a scream had him sitting up in bed, shaking.

"Probably a mountain lion," he told himself when his heart stopped thumping.

Maybe that's what it was. But down in Kirby the train had come through and stopped for water. It was a while before it got started again. A woman had been standing on the tracks. The engineer didn't see her until it was too late.

In the morning, the marshal came by to tell Hartley about the accident. No doubt about it, the dead woman was Molly.

"Maybe she was running out to catch the train," the marshal said. But he thought that maybe Molly was so upset that she wanted the train to hit her.

That night Hartley went out to dinner. The first thing he saw when he got home was Molly's suitcase standing in the hall. Somebody —

maybe that fool marshal — must have left it there. Well, he didn't want it. He'd get rid of it somehow, but not right now. He shoved it into the little closet under the stairs.

It was late, but he felt restless. He sat down at the desk in the den and began to go through the old man's papers. But he couldn't concentrate. The house seemed to make so much noise. Windows rattled. Stairs creaked. Twice he went out to the entrance hallway because he thought he heard someone walking up and down. But there was no one there.

About an hour later he heard a new sound. It was the slow creak of rusty hinges on an opening door. He jumped up again and went to the hallway. The door to the closet under the stairs was half open.

"I know I latched that," he said out loud. But he couldn't help looking in the closet. It was a strange relief to see the suitcase still there. He slammed the door shut and latched it.

No doubt about it, this place was getting on his nerves. He'd go outside and get a breath of cold air. He walked up and down the long veranda for a while, and then went back inside.

The closet door was open again. This time there was no suitcase inside.

It seemed to Hartley as if the house was holding its breath, waiting to see what he would do next. Slowly and carefully, like an old man, he went upstairs.

The door to the room Molly had used was

open, too. At the foot of her bed the suitcase lay open. Neatly-folded clothes were laid out on the bed, just as if she was unpacking after a long journey.

"Whoever is doing this expects me to start screaming and run away," Hartley told himself. "But I'm not going to do it. I'm going to find out which friend of Molly's is trying to scare me away. And when I find out, I'm going to send that friend to jail!"

He looked in every closet on the second floor. Then he checked out the first floor, then the basement. He couldn't find a living soul.

By morning he was exhausted. But he didn't dare try to sleep until the sun came up.

The second night was like the first one. The house made odd noises. Hartley took Molly's clothes down to the furnace and burned them. Then he walked around, trying to decide which of Molly's friends was giving him such a hard time. It had to be someone who knew her, because Hartley didn't believe in ghosts.

By morning he was pale and shaky. Then he smelled fresh coffee brewing. It smelled so good that he didn't stop to wonder who could be making it.

The smell was coming from the kitchen. He almost ran there, but stopped short at the door. Coffee was steaming in a cup on the table. Bacon, eggs, and toast were hot on a plate.

Whomever the prankster was, he didn't mean to starve. Hartley was grinning as he sat down and picked up a fork. Then he put the fork down. Suppose the food was poisoned. Suppose Molly's friend meant to kill him.

And that's the way it went on for the next two days. Food would be set out in the kitchen three times a day. Hartley never caught whoever was doing it. He never ate it, either. But he couldn't help noticing that somehow the dishes were mysteriously washed and put away between meals.

The nights were the worst. At two in the morning, he would hear the train whistle over at Kirby. Then he would hear the scream! Hartley sat wrapped in a blanket in the den and told himself he was going to go hunting for that mountain lion. In the meantime, he was going to telephone the marshal and have him come up and search the house. About sunrise that's just what he did.

Later, the marshal tried to make sense out of what happened. "I never saw a man so changed in a few days," he said. "When I got to the house, he looked as if he had aged at least 20 years. He told me some pal of Molly's was hiding in the house, trying to drive him crazy.

"Well, I started taking off my coat, and he started upstairs. 'I'm going to lie down awhile,' he told me. 'You search every inch of this place. I want whoever it is arrested for trespassing.'

"All of a sudden the whole house started to shake. It was like being in an earthquake. I was knocked right off my feet.

"Hartley was at the top of the stairs, holding

tight to the bannister. The house shook harder. The nails came out of the railing. I could hear them falling on the floor. Then the whole bannister just fell apart, and Hartley fell down. Broke his neck. . . ."

Hartley was the last person to try to live in the Muldoon house. Even tramps stayed away from it. It had some fine old furniture in it, but nobody ever tried to steal it. If you asked people around there why, they'd say, "It wouldn't be right. Molly wouldn't like it."

———————————————

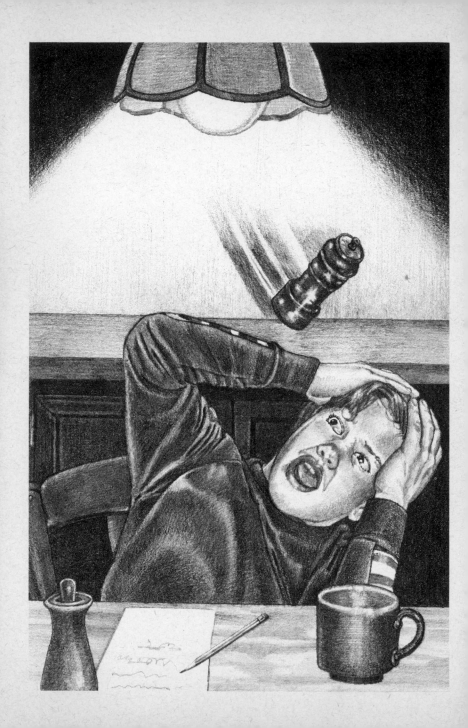

The Haunted Apartment

Picture a haunted house. It should be old, right? With blank, staring windows and plenty of cobwebs? And a convenient graveyard nearby?

Now picture a haunted apartment. It has four large, airy rooms, and it's in a housing development in Newark, N.J. Instead of a graveyard, there's a playground nearby.

In 1960, Mrs. Maybelle Clark and her grandson, Ernie, moved into an apartment in a housing development in Newark. At first, things couldn't have been more pleasant. Then came Ernie's 13th birthday — and trouble!

"I was getting supper ready," says Mrs. Clark, "and Ernie was doing his homework at the kitchen table. I saw it was six o'clock, and I said, 'Well, Ernie, this is the hour you were born. Now you're officially 13 years old.

"Just at that moment, a big pepper mill I keep on a high shelf floated into the air. It circled Ernie's head, and then set itself gently down on the table beside him.

"We just stared at it with our mouths open. There was no way we could know that was the last peaceful moment we would have for weeks."

Mrs. Clark was so right. The trouble *really* started the next morning at breakfast. As Ernie sat down, the dishes on the table flew into the air and smashed against the walls. Light bulbs in the overhead fixture popped.

"I yelled to Ernie to get out, to go to school! I was afraid he might be hit by one of those plates and get hurt. The minute he left, everything got quiet. By the time I had cleaned up the mess, I had gotten over being scared," Mrs. Clark recalls.

But the barrage was far from over. When Ernie got home from school, the crockery began to fly again. A lamp jumped off a living room table and smashed at his feet. Glasses left the kitchen drainboard and shattered in midair as he ran by. Terrified, the boy dived under the bed and refused to come out.

"He spent a good part of the night there, and I don't think he slept much," says Mrs. Clark. "Things quieted down at about two A.M. But I couldn't relax. I lay there turning it over and over in my mind. Why was this happening to us? It didn't make sense."

Mrs. Clark tried to beat the jinx by packing what was left of her dishes and glasswear in crates. Just to be on the safe side, she nailed the crates up and stowed them away in a closet. She bought paper plates and cups, and used them for their meals. For almost a week her precautions seemed to be working.

"Ernie and I didn't exactly forget what had happened, but we relaxed a little bit. But then there was that Friday night. Ernie went from school to a basketball game. I was watching television when he came home."

What happened next was like a nightmare. The television screen went black. A high-pitched whistle seemed to come from the set. Then the closet door burst open and one of the packing crates sailed out into the room. The nails Mrs. Clark had pounded in so carefully popped out. Once more flying plates, saucers, and cups filled the air — only to smash to the floor. An iron, its cord trailing like a comet, whizzed by and crashed through the window.

For Mrs. Clark, it was also the breaking point. The neighbors were complaining. The landlord wanted her to move.

"Can't somebody help us?" she sobbed to a newspaper reporter.

It turned out that somebody could. Dr. Charles

Wrege, a psychologist who taught at New York University, offered to try to get to the bottom of the trouble.

Dr. Wrege moved into the Clark apartment. He checked every object and piece of furniture to make sure there was no trickery. He talked to Ernie for a long time. He was soon convinced the boy wasn't using any physical force to make objects move.

What Dr. Wrege suspected was that the boy and his grandmother were being haunted by a *poltergeist* — a German word that means "stone-throwing ghost." Poltergeists are said to be noisy, mischievous spirits. Unlike most ghosts, they are never seen. But they are certainly heard. They're the practical jokers of the spirit world, but few poltergeist victims enjoy their jokes.

While Dr. Wrege investigated the apartment, crowds gathered outside. They had come to see "the boy who makes things fly." Next, the police came to break up the crowds. At that moment a canister of salt flew out of the kitchen and grazed Ernie's head!

The canister was the last thing the Clark poltergeist threw. Maybe the crowds scared it away. Maybe the attention poor Ernie was getting was enough to satisfy any spook. But the Clark poltergeist will always be one of a kind. It was the first case of a haunting ever reported from a housing development.

The Playroom

In the 1920s, Rawlins, Wyoming, was a small town. It didn't have a high school or a city park. But it had an unusual number of mansions — big, expensive houses that wouldn't have been out of place in London, Boston, or New York. These houses had been built by people who made a lot of money in oil, sheep, and cattle.

Ethel Shelby had dreams of living in one of these houses. It was a scaled-down version of an English countryhouse, and its landscaped grounds were like a small park. It was surrounded by a high wrought-iron fence that Ethel spent a lot of time peering through.

The house was for sale, but there was no chance of the Shelbys moving into it. Ethel's father worked in an oil refinery in the nearby town of Parco. The dingy white frame house off Front Street was the best he could afford.

The family had moved to Rawlins two years before, when Ethel was 10. Being shy, she had made no friends. Besides, there was no hope of bringing a friend home because her brother, Will, was always sick. He hadn't been able to get out of bed for months, and lately the doctor came more and more often.

When summer came and school was out, Ethel tried to help her mother. She offered to read to Will or play cards with him. But her mother shooed her away.

"Will's just not up to it today, dear," she'd say. "Maybe tomorrow. Why don't you finish the dishes and then go take a walk. You should try to find children your own age to play with — and you won't find them by moping around here."

Ethel did as she was told. As was usual on any walk she took, she soon found herself by the wrought-iron fence. As usual, she stopped and looked through the bars at her dream house. That was how she happened to see Roy for the first time.

At the back of the big house, making a right angle to it, was what some people called a "carriage house." Once horses had been kept in the downstairs part, and the groom had lived on the second floor. Now the carriage house could be used as a garage, and no one lived upstairs. Yet one of the upper windows was opening. A boy

was leaning out. He waved at her.

"Come on up," he called.

Ethel stared, and he waved again. Hesitantly, she opened the iron gates and went inside. The boy was still hanging out the window when she got to the carriage house.

"Don't be scared," he told her. "My name is Roy. What's yours?"

"Ethel Shelby. Do you live here?"

He nodded. "Sometimes. I've got a playroom up here. But it's lonesome because I'm not around here much. I haven't got any friends."

"I know how that feels," Ethel said.

Roy grinned at her. "Then how about coming up here?"

Once upstairs, Ethel felt as if she were dreaming. The big loft was crammed with toys of all kinds. An electric train set covered half the floor. Dust-covered books and games were piled in the corners.

"Where's your family?" Ethel asked.

"Oh, they're all away. I'm only here for the summer."

"But there's no housekeeper. The house is up for sale. What do you do about meals and clean clothes and things?"

"Oh, those things are all taken care of."

For the next six weeks, Ethel spent at least part of every day at the carriage house. She and Roy talked, played games, and played with the toys. It was the happiest time she had ever had.

Her new-found happiness kept her from noticing her parents' strained, anxious faces. And they were too busy with Will to wonder where she was spending her time.

Once in a while she realized how little she knew about Roy. It was hard to find out anything.

"Don't your parents worry about your being here alone?" she asked.

He shook his head. "Don't yours?"

"I guess not," said Ethel. "All they seem to think about is my brother. He's been sick a long time. Now he can't even sit up in bed."

"What's his name? How old is he?"

"William. He's 13. Can I take him one of these toys?"

"No, not now. I'll save one for him. What would he like?"

"The train. He's always wanted an electric train. If the train's too much, maybe he could have one of the cars." She stopped and a quaver came into her voice. "Maybe he won't ever get well enough to play with it."

Roy smiled. "I promise you he'll play with the whole train. Did I ever tell you I could see into the future? I see Will up here, playing with the train."

Ethel stared at him. "Really? No, you're making fun of me. Will's really sick. I'd better go now. I'll come back tomorrow."

But it was two weeks before she came back. Will died the next day. At the funeral Ethel heard people saying "leukemia." She didn't know what it meant.

Things were even worse at home. Her mother didn't even seem to notice her, and her father was away at work.

One morning Ethel realized she hadn't seen Roy for a long time. He didn't even know what had happened to Will. With a start, she realized he had promised Will wouldn't die. She would go and tell him how wrong he had been.

Before she left the house, she crept into Will's

room. The watch he had gotten for Christmas was in the drawer of the table by the bed. She slipped it into her pocket.

As she went through the iron gates, she heard laughter coming from the carriage house. When she started up the stairs, she could hear the sound of the electric train running.

Suddenly Roy appeared at the top of the stairs.

"What do you want?" he asked sharply.

"I just came to see you. I've got lots to tell you. And look, I brought you a present." She held out the watch.

"I don't need a watch. And I don't need you." He moved to stand between her and the door to the playroom. "I've got a new friend now. Don't come here anymore."

He gave her a little push toward the stairs. Then he ducked inside the room and slammed the door. But he wasn't quite quick enough. She got a glimpse of the inside of the room.

Ethel ran all the way home, shuddering and sobbing. She burst into the house and grabbed her mother's arm. "Mama, Will's not dead! He's over at the Wilkerson house. He's playing with Roy's electric train. I saw him!"

Mrs. Shelby stared at her daughter. "Ethel, what are you saying? You know Will is dead. You were at his funeral. What are you talking about?"

"He's in the playroom, the playroom over the carriage house. Roy has lots of toys up there. And now he's got Will . . ."

Mrs. Shelby called the doctor and made Ethel go to bed. The doctor said Ethel's outburst was caused by delayed shock and grief. He gave her a shot to make her sleep.

As she drifted off, she heard her mother say, "Who is this Roy? I thought the Wilkerson place was up for sale."

"It is," said the doctor. "There's no one living there at the present. The only Roy I know about was Mr. Wilkerson's younger brother. But he died a long time ago of diptheria. He was only a kid. There hasn't been a child living in the Wilkerson place since then. . . ."

———————————

Ghosts
<u>Along the Road</u>

Not all spooks have houses to haunt. Some seem to prefer an afterlife out-of-doors. Others are wanderers who don't seem too sure about where they belong.

On a summer afternoon in 1958, Tom Welford was driving along a road outside Honolulu. Heat rose in shimmering waves from the dusty highway. Up ahead on the road, Tom saw what at first appeared to be a large, wavery red blot. As he got closer, the blot took on the shape of a young woman in a red dress.

She stepped out in the road right in front of his car. He jammed on the brakes and stopped.

"That was a stupid thing to do!" he yelled. "You could get killed. What do you want — a lift into Honolulu?"

She shook her head. "No, thank you. Can you tell me how to get to the Hawaiian Village Hotel in Honolulu? Can you write the directions for me on this paper?"

She reached in through the window and handed him a piece of yellow notepaper. He shrugged and wrote down the directions of the hotel. She took the paper, thanked him, and he drove away.

He thought it strange that she refused a lift because he was going to the same hotel himself. But when he mentioned this to her, she only shook her head again.

It was late afternoon when he reached the hotel. As he was signing the register, the manager handed him a piece of yellow notepaper. "A young lady left this message for you, Mr. Welford."

Puzzled, Tom unfolded the paper. On it were the directions he had written for the woman in the road.

"I don't understand," Tom said. "Wasn't there a note with this?"

The manager was staring at him oddly. "No note, Mr. Welford. And there is something we don't understand about the young lady. We were hoping you could explain it."

The manager beckoned to one of the bellboys, who hurried over. "Tell Mr. Welford what happened with the young lady in the red dress," he ordered.

Tom could see that the boy looked shaken. "I can't explain it, sir. I was told to take the young lady up to her room after she registered. She didn't have any luggage. We got on an empty elevator, and went straight up. But when the elevator stopped, she wasn't there! She had just vanished. I couldn't believe it, so I went right back down to the lobby. Nobody there had seen her. I can't understand it."

"I can't either," said Tom. "I met the girl on the road this afternoon and wrote out the directions for her. But I don't even know her name — and she didn't know mine! Yet she found out who I was and left this message for me."

Suddenly a thought struck him. "You said she registered," he told the manager. "Her name and address must be in your records, then."

The manager swung the heavy register book around so Tom could look at it. The line he pointed to was blank. Yet there were names written on the lines above and below it.

The mystery of the young woman in the red dress has haunted Tom ever since. He checked with the Honolulu police, but no one of that description had been reported missing.

"It's as if she never existed," says Tom. "But if she doesn't really exist, how could the manager, the bellboy, and I all have seen and talked to her on the same day?"

When it comes to ghosts, there are always

"how" questions. How can you be walking along near Powell and Jones Streets in San Francisco — and have a young woman walk right *through* you? Many people have reported this over the years. They say the woman is about 18, pretty, and wears a long, white, old-fashioned dress. She smiles at everyone she passes.

"She looks solid and real," said one witness. "But if you don't get out of her way, you feel a sudden wave of cold — and there she is, on the other side of you — and you know she didn't walk around you!"

The woman in white has been seen by San Franciscans since the 1880s. She even has a name — "Flora of Nob Hill." She is supposed to be the ghost of Flora Summerton.

The Summertons were wealthy and lived in the part of San Francisco known as Nob Hill. They saw no reason why their only daughter shouldn't marry the rich man they had chosen for her — even if he was old enough to be her father. But Flora rebelled. One evening in 1876, she set out for a ball, wearing a long white gown. Her parents never saw her again.

For months, police hunted for Flora. A reward of $250,000 was offered for her return. But the years passed with no news of her.

Where did she go? To Butte, Montana, where she worked as a housekeeper in a hotel. It was only after she died in 1926 that her real identity was discovered. Her employer opened a trunk in

her room. Inside was her birth certificate — and a long white ball gown.

Hitchhiking is dangerous, but not for the young woman drivers often see on the Archer Road in Chicago. Rain or shine, she appears and hitches rides. But drivers who pick her up have a surprise in store. When they pass the old Resurrection Cemetery, they discover she is no longer in the car.

One driver was so upset by this experience that he went to the police. Then asked him to describe the woman. They they showed him a photograph from their files.

"That's her!" he said. "Who is she? Has she got a record or something?"

"Yes, but not the kind of record you mean. The record says that she was killed in a car crash in 1931. She was coming home from a dance, poor kid. A lot of drivers have reported picking her up — then having her vanish. We call her Resurrection Mary. She always vanishes when she gets to the place where she's buried — Resurrection Cemetery."

There's another graveyard in Chicago which has an even stranger ghost.

The road that leads to Bachelor Grove Cemetery is a peaceful one. The old-fashioned house near the cemetery gates is peaceful looking, too. It's a comfortable looking place, with four columns at the entrance and a porch swing. In the evening, a soft glow of light comes through its windows.

There are problems with the house. Sometimes it's on one side of the road. Sometimes it's on the other. It can move about easily because it's not really there. It's proof that not all ghosts are people. This ghost is a house!

Those who have seen the ghost house report that it looks very solid. But no one has yet gotten out of a car and knocked on the door of the house. Suppose it opened . . . ?

———————————

Haunted Houses You Can Visit

Even if you don't believe in ghosts, it's fun to visit houses that other people believe are haunted. In the list below you will find famous haunted houses that are open to the public. These houses are historical places, listed by the U.S. Department of Commerce. If you happen to be in the neighborhood and want to visit any of them, get in touch with the local Chamber of Commerce. They will tell you what the visiting hours are.

If none of these haunted houses happen to be in your town, don't feel left out. Write your local Chamber of Commerce, and ask them if they know of a nearby haunted house you can visit.

NAME OF HOUSE	LOCATION	GHOSTLY GOINGS-ON
CALIFORNIA		
Whaley House	San Diego	Four noisy ghosts hang out here. Footsteps and the rustle of silken clothes are heard. Cigar smoke is often smelled.

WASHINGTON D.C.

United States Capitol	Washington, D.C.	Haunted by a "demon cat" plus the ghosts of John Quincy Adams and Pierre L'Enfant.
White House	Washington, D.C.	The ghosts of Abraham Lincoln and Dolly Madison have been reported here.
Decatur House	Washington, D.C.	Stephen Decatur, the original owner, died in a duel. His ghost is still said to be "at home."
Octagon House	Washington, D.C.	The ghosts here are female, and there are two of them.

DELAWARE

Woodburn House	Dover	One spirit here doesn't care for spirits. It empties out wine decanters and shows up on stair landings. Spirits are also said to lurk in the "Haunted Tree" in front of the house. This house is also the Governor's Mansion.

LOUISIANA

The Cottage Plantation	Baton Rouge	A ruined, burned-out shell, said to be haunted by a man's ghost.
Oakland Manor	Franklin	White-pillared mansion haunted by the ghost of politician Henry Clay.

Lloyd's Hall	Meeker	A ghostly musician plays the violin from the second-floor porch. Blood stains keep turning up on the third floor.
St. Maurice Plantation	Natchitoches	In the house, spirits turn book pages. On the grounds, a child's ghost rises from the cemetery when the moon is full, and dances in the pasture.
Beauregard House	New Orleans	The ghost of Civil War General P.T.G. Beauregard has been seen fighting a spirited battle in the upper hallway.
Madame Lalaurie House	New Orleans	Screams have been heard from the roof. It is said to be haunted by the ghosts of murdered slaves.
Farlange Plantation	New Roads	The ghost of a pretty girl floats through this pretty place.
The Myrtles Plantation	St. Francisville	Oldest and biggest plantation in the state. Haunted by the ghost of a French governess who peers into the faces of sleepers in the bedrooms.

MARYLAND

USA CONSTELLATION	Baltimore	This ship, now a floating museum, is haunted by the ghost of a sailor killed in 1799. He triggers the bur-

glar alarm and sits in the gun ports. It is said he returns to clear his name of charges of cowardice.

MAINE

Musical Wonder House and Antique Shop	Wiscassett	Spirits chatter and move the furniture around here.

PENNSYLVANIA

Loudoun Mansion	Germantown	A 19th-century merchant built this house. It's haunted by the spirit of an eight-year-old boy, who plays tricks on the guides.
	New Hope	Every building in this town is said to be haunted, but the folks who live there don't mind.

VIRGINIA

Ramsay House	Alexandria	The house ghost appears at an upstairs window. It is said to be the ghost of William Ramsay.
Robert E. Lee Home	Alexandria	The ghost of a little boy and a spook dog haunt here. Many think the child is Robert E. Lee as a boy.
Haw Branch Plantation	Amelia	Ghostly scents of roses and oranges, plus a haunted portrait and a mysterious "Lady in White" spook.

Scotchtown	near Ashland	Dolly Madison once lived here. So did Patrick Henry. It's haunted by a lady ghost, and dueling spirits who leave bloodstains in the hall.
Westover Plantation	Charles City	Evelyn Byrd died here of a broken heart. Her father wouldn't let her marry the man she loved. Now her ghost roams the garden.
Shirley Plantation	Charles City County (near Malven Hill)	A portrait of a character called "Aunt Pratt" makes ghostly noises and causes chairs to rock.
Kenmore	Fredericksburg	Colonel Fielding Lewis lived here during the Revolutionary War. He loved it so much that his ghost still haunts his former bedroom.
Belle Grove	Middletown	There are said to be ghosts in the smokehouse and the spirit of a murdered woman roaming the plantation.
Wyth House	Williamsburg	Lady Skipworth once lived in this 18th-century house. Her ghost, dressed in a ball gown, floats about the place.

Author's Note

Are the stories in this book really true? The answer is yes. Everything you read here really happened to real people. Some of the stories come from newspaper clippings. Some were told to me by the people they happened to. I lived near the cottage on Clarkson Street, and I also lived in Rawlins, Wyoming, when the incident described in "The Playroom" took place.

Are there really ghosts? Some people think so. Others say there must be a logical explanation for all these unsolved mysteries. I don't know whether or not I believe in ghosts, but I do know many strange things have happened that nobody has yet been able to explain. I have always been interested in these happenings, and have spent years collecting stories about them.

It may be that you are one of those who don't believe in ghosts. I hope you enjoyed this book anyway, just for fun. Tales of the weird and unexplained may seem like nonsense to you, but you'll have to admit they're fun to read about.

— **M.R.**

Practice Shelf-Hypnosis!

Cast a bright spell over your bookshelves and
turn your book collection from dull to Dynamite!
Collect the complete set of Dynamite Books.

Magic Wanda's Dynamite Magic Book
Count Morbida's Dynamite Puzzle Book
The Dynamite Party Book
The Dynamite Book of Top Secret Information
The Dynamite Monster Hall of Fame
The Dynamite Book of Bummers
The Officially Official Dynamite Club Handbook
The Dynamite Year-Round Catalog of Hot Stuff
The Dynamite People Book
Count Morbida's Fang-tastic Activity Book
Gotcha! The Dynamite Book of Sneaky Tricks,
Silly Jokes, and Harmless Pranks To Play On Your Friend
A Laugh and a Half: The Dynamite Book of Funny Stuff
The Dynamite 3-D Poster Book
The Dynamite Do-It-Yourself Pen Pal Kit
Good Vibrations: Straight Talk and Solid Advice for Kids
The Dynamite Animal Hall of Fame
The Dynamite Kids' Guide to the Movies
Dynamite's Funny Book of the Sad Facts of Life
The Dynamite Book of Ghosts and Haunted Houses
Count Morbida's Monster Quiz Book